Grammaropolis

PRESENTS

Meet the Parts of Speech

8

POPULATION

Student Workbook

FOURTH GRADE

written by
THE MAYOR OF GRAMMAROPOLIS

HOUSTON

T0169339

Edited by Christopher Knight
Cover and Interior Design by Mckee Frazior
Character Design by Powerhouse Animation

ISBN: 9781644420331
Copyright © 2020 by Grammaropolis LLC
Illustrations copyright © 2020 by Grammaropolis LLC
All rights reserved.
Published by Grammaropolis
Distributed by Six Foot Press
Printed in the U.S.A.

Grammaropolis.com
Six Foot Press.com

Table of Contents

Table of Contents

> For information on how Grammaropolis correlates to state standards,
> please visit us online at edu.grammaropolis.com.

FROM THE DESK OF THE MAYOR

There's a reason students can instantly recall everything that happened in their favorite movies but struggle to retain much of the important information you're trying to cover in school: people are hard-wired to remember what we connect with on an emotional level.

That's why grammar is so hard to teach. (As a former grammar teacher myself, I know firsthand.) Traditional materials are dry, abstract, and lifeless. There's nothing to connect with. Put simply, grammar is boring.

But it doesn't have to be! Our story-based approach combines traditional instruction with original narrative content, appealing to different learning styles and encouraging students to make a deeper connection with the elements of grammar.

In Grammaropolis, adverbs don't just modify verbs; adverbs are bossy! They tell the verbs **where** to go, **when** to leave, and **how** to get there. A pronoun doesn't just replace a noun; Roger the pronoun is a shady character who's always trying to trick Nelson the noun into giving up his spot.

And it works! Our mobile apps have already been downloaded over 2.5 million times, and thousands of schools and districts use our web-based site license. In other words, we don't skimp on the vegetables; we just make them taste good.

Thanks so much for visiting Grammaropolis. I hope you enjoy your stay!

– The Mayor

Meet the Parts of Speech!

Nouns

name a person, place, thing, or idea.

Verbs

express action or a state of being.

Adverbs

modify a verb, an adjective, or another adverb.

Adjectives

modify a noun or pronoun.

Prepositions

show a logical relationship or locate an object in time or space.

Pronouns

take the place of one or more nouns or pronouns.

Interjections

express strong or mild emotion.

Conjunctions

join words or word groups.

Grammaropolis

Meet the Nouns!

EXAMPLES

PERSON: <u>Keyshawn</u> is my best <u>friend</u>.

PLACE: Val has always dreamed of visiting <u>Argentina</u>.

THING: Brian's <u>order</u> of <u>doughnuts</u> came in a large <u>box</u>.

IDEA: <u>Practice</u> helps you overcome your <u>fear</u> of <u>failure</u>.

Common Nouns and Proper Nouns

Common Nouns

Sheldon is my <u>cousin</u>.
His <u>shoes</u> were made by Nike.

Proper Nouns

<u>Sheldon</u> is my cousin.
His shoes were made by <u>Nike</u>.

Pro Tip:
A noun that names a general person, place, thing, or idea is called a **common noun**.

Pro Tip:
A noun that names a specific person, place, thing, or idea is called a **proper noun**.

Let's Practice!

Instructions:
In each of the following sentences, circle any common nouns and underline any proper nouns.

EXAMPLE:
That dog is a Labrador Retriever, and Ryan is its owner.

1. I would love it if we could go to Dairy Queen after school on Monday.

2. Giles told the class a story about how he tripped on the curb on Main Street.

3. My dentist told me not to worry about cavities for some reason.

4. Microsoft is a company that makes software and game consoles.

5. Rex, Amy, and Pilar came over to my house to watch a movie.

Your turn!

Instructions:
Write a sentence that includes at least one proper noun, a sentence that includes at least one common noun, and a sentence that includes at least one of each. Circle the common nouns and underline the proper nouns.

1. proper _____

2. common _____

3. one of each _____

Concrete Nouns and Abstract Nouns

Concrete Nouns
Julian drove his car to school to pick up his books.

Abstract Nouns
Julian has honor and integrity, so he never cheats.

FIVE SENSES

Pro Tip:
A *concrete noun* names a person, place, or thing that can be perceived by one or more of the five senses.

Pro Tip:
An *abstract noun* names an idea or quality that cannot be perceived by any of the five senses.

Let's Practice!

Instructions:
In each of the following sentences, circle any concrete nouns and underline any abstract nouns.

EXAMPLE:
My dog has many great qualities, but my favorite is his loyalty.

1. A sense of worry filled the room when we started to smell smoke.

2. Some people chase power, but my best friend never seems to care about it.

3. Alton didn't watch the movie about snakes because he has a strong fear of them.

4. I'll order a large cup of coffee and a small doughnut, please.

5. My parents don't appreciate my stubbornness, which they call willfulness.

Your turn!

Instructions:
Write a sentence that includes at least one concrete noun, a sentence that includes at least one abstract noun, and a sentence that includes at least one of each. Circle the concrete nouns and underline the abstract nouns.

1. concrete _____

2. abstract _____

3. one of each _____

Grammaropolis

Collective Nouns

My neighbor's cat just gave birth to the cutest <u>litter</u> of kittens you have ever seen.

Willie chopped an entire <u>cord</u> of firewood and then opened a new <u>pack</u> of gum as a reward.

Pro Tip:
A *collective noun* is a singular noun that names a group.

Let's practice!

Instructions:
Circle all of the collective nouns in the each of the following sentences.

EXAMPLE:
My (class) has only twenty-five students now that the Wight twins moved away.

1. You can call it a herd or a drove, but all I know is that's a lot of cattle!

2. I peered into the audience until I finally found my brother's smiling face.

3. Kwame gave Sandra the prettiest bouquet of flowers anyone has ever seen.

4. Carlos's favorite possessions are his coin collection and an old anthology of poems.

5. There's nothing quite like a tall stack of pancakes with butter and syrup.

Your turn!

Instructions:
Use the collective nouns below to write your very own sentences.

1. set _____

2. band _____

3. bunch _____

Compound Nouns

Kevin bought his **step-brother** a toy **spaceship** as a **birthday** present.

Pro Tip:
*A **compound noun** is formed when two or more words combine to make a single noun. A compound noun can be one single word, two words, or words connected by hyphens.*

Let's practice!

Instructions:
Circle all of the compound nouns in each of the following sentences.

EXAMPLE:
Some people like (hot dogs) and (cheeseburgers,) but my (great-grandfather) prefers salad.

1. Lori's favorite waterfall is just on the other side of the railroad.

2. The baby sat in her highchair licking fresh honeycomb from the beehive.

3. Valerie is very good at carving jack-o-lanterns with her pocketknife.

4. My mom can't eat pineapple anymore because it hurts her mouth.

5. I know that Les stole my lunchbox because Les's fingerprints are all over it.

Your turn!

Instructions:
Create your own compound nouns by adding another word to the words below.

dog	_____	high	_____
sun	_____	lunch	_____
pine	_____	down	_____
road	_____	sand	_____

Singular Nouns and Plural Nouns

Name:

Singular Nouns
I stubbed my <u>toe</u> on a chair <u>leg</u>, and now my <u>foot</u> hurts.

Plural Nouns
My <u>feet</u> always hurt when I stub my <u>toes</u> on chair <u>legs</u>.

Pro Tip:
A **singular noun** names a single person, place, thing, or idea.
A **plural noun** names more than one person, place, thing, or idea.

Pro Tip:
Most nouns are made plural by adding -s, or -es to the singular form. The ones that don't are called **irregular** plural nouns.

Let's Practice!

Instructions:
In each of the following sentences, circle any singular nouns and underline any plural nouns.

EXAMPLE:
This is a fun fact that my sister just told me: baby geese are called goslings.

1. That shelf is only for my favorite books, but the other shelves are for any books.

2. Some people never turn off the lights when they go to bed at night.

3. Larry was careful when he lit those matches, so he didn't start a fire.

4. Bridget is the name of my favorite sheep, but I don't know what those sheep are named.

5. I just ate a bowl of cacti and potatoes, and there was really more than one cactus in it.

Your turn!

Instructions:
Turn the following singular nouns into plural nouns. Remember that some might be irregular!

kiss _____   tomato _____

knife _____   loaf _____

tooth _____   wolf _____

volcano _____   quiz _____

Writing with Nouns

INSTRUCTIONS (PART ONE):
Brainstorm some of your favorite nouns for each of the following categories.

PROPER	COMMON	ABSTRACT	COLLECTIVE	COMPOUND
-----------------	-----------------	-----------------	-----------------	-----------------
-----------------	-----------------	-----------------	-----------------	-----------------
-----------------	-----------------	-----------------	-----------------	-----------------
-----------------	-----------------	-----------------	-----------------	-----------------

INSTRUCTIONS (PART TWO):
Now use as many of the above nouns as you can to write a short story. Don't forget to circle the nouns when you use them!

_____

_____

_____

_____

_____

_____

Grammaropolis

The Big Noun Quiz!

INSTRUCTIONS: Classify the noun type for the <u>underlined nouns</u> below from among the available options.

1. After dinner, my dad sits in his <u>armchair</u> and reads for an hour.
   ○ abstract   ○ collective   ○ proper   ○ compound

2. Does anyone around here have a fresh <u>deck</u> of cards that we could use?
   ○ abstract   ○ collective   ○ proper   ○ compound

3. I don't think it's possible for <u>Mr. Salazar</u> to ever stop smiling.
   ○ abstract   ○ collective   ○ proper   ○ compound

4. Whenever Julie is about to feed her dog, he bounces with hopeful <u>anticipation</u>.
   ○ abstract   ○ collective   ○ proper   ○ compound

5. My aunt keeps an enormous stack of magazines on her <u>nightstand</u>.
   ○ abstract   ○ collective   ○ proper   ○ compound

INSTRUCTIONS: Indicate whether the <u>underlined nouns</u> below are singular or plural nouns.

6. My dentist said that she really wants me to brush my <u>teeth</u> even more than I do now.
   ○ singular   ○ plural

7. The farmer looked up to see two <u>wolves</u> pacing eagerly around the fence line.
   ○ singular   ○ plural

8. The Wildcats are my favorite <u>team</u> in the whole league.
   ○ singular   ○ plural

9. Peter asked the clerk to give him some <u>loaves</u> of bread.
   ○ singular   ○ plural

10. Taylor is one of the most talented <u>women</u> I have ever seen.
    ○ singular   ○ plural

Grammaropolis

Meet the Verbs!

I am an action verb!

I express action.

EXAMPLES

Billy **joined** a club.
I **disagree** with your answer.
Sasha **will greet** the guests.

I am a linking verb.

I express a state of being.

EXAMPLES

Those people **were** interesting.
I **am** a big fan of yours.
Something in here **smells** fishy.

Grammaropolis

Action Verbs Express Action

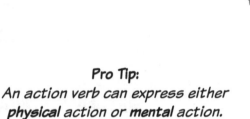

Physical Action
Felipe **jumped** into the mountain lake!

Mental Action
I **hope** that you **will remember** me!

Pro Tip:
An action verb can express either **physical** action or **mental** action.

Let's practice!

Instructions:
Circle the action verb in each of the following sentences and indicate whether it is expressing physical or mental action.

EXAMPLE:

I really (need) a good grade in this class.   ___mental action___

1. We will perform the monologues from our play tomorrow. _____

2. Henry simply guessed the last answer on the test.   _____

3. Jake turned onto my street at exactly midnight.   _____

4. Gil and his sister thought about lunch all day.   _____

5. Felix painted an enormous circle on the side of the barn. _____

Your turn!

Instructions:
Write sentences using your own action verbs to express mental or physical action as indicated. Don't forget to circle the action verb you use!

1. physical _____

2. mental _____

3. physical _____

Grammaropolis

Transitive Action Verbs

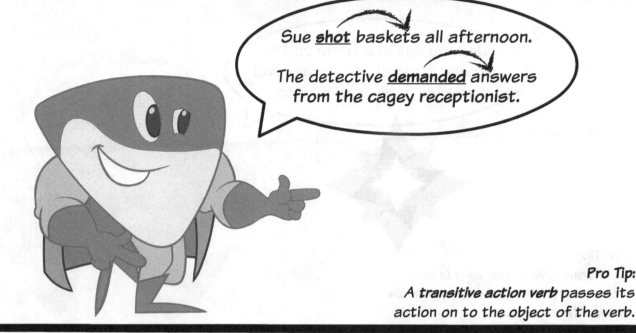

Sue **shot** baskets all afternoon.

The detective **demanded** answers from the cagey receptionist.

Pro Tip:
A *transitive action verb* passes its action on to the object of the verb.

Let's Practice!

Instructions:
Circle any transitive action verbs in each sentence and draw arrows to their objects.

EXAMPLE:
Zeke baked a big vanilla cake and ate the whole thing!

1. If you open the door tonight, you will catch a view of the parade.

2. We have to watch our language whenever we play soccer in the park.

3. Shut the window before you catch a cold!

4. This new product will eliminate its competition.

5. Lev will accept your answer only if you first compare your work with his.

Your turn!

Instructions:
Write sentences with the verbs below as transitive action verbs. Don't forget to circle the verbs and draw arrows to their objects.

1. save _____

2. burn _____

3. follow _____

Intransitive Action Verbs

Joanna **sat** in a room on the second floor of the library and **studied** in blissful silence.

Pro Tip:
*An **intransitive action verb** is an action verb that does not pass its action to an object.*

Let's Practice!

Instructions:
Circle the intransitive action verb in each of the following sentences.

EXAMPLE:
I usually (jog) for a while, and then I (sprint) from one end of the street to the other.

1. After we played in the sun, we relaxed and slept in the shade.

2. Kyle wandered all around the neighborhood, and nobody followed.

3. Granny laughed and smiled as she pointed in my direction.

4. Stephen and Lila disagree on some of the most important aspects of the plan.

5. Some people whistle while they work.

Your turn!

Instructions:
Write sentences using the verbs below as intransitive action verbs. Don't forget to circle the action verbs in the sentences!

1. speak _____

2. walk _____

3. fall _____

Linking Verbs Express a State of Being

Name:

Linking verbs express a state of being. They "link" the subject to information that renames the subject.

"To be":
You <u>were</u> invited.
Bobbie <u>is</u> a firefighter.

Pro Tip:
Linking verbs often take a form of the verb "**to be**" but they don't have to!

Not "to be":
Carl <u>looked</u> upset.
That <u>smells</u> amazing.

Let's practice!

Instructions:
Circle the linking verb in each of the following sentences.

EXAMPLE:
Henry and his dog (are) excited for the cupcake festival.

1. The day turned dark during the eclipse.

2. This restaurant will be such a good addition to the neighborhood.

3. Mr. Center's famous peach cobbler tastes a little stale today.

4. We will become best friends this year.

5. David's little brother sounds upset for some reason.

Your turn!

Instructions:
Write three sentences using your own linking verbs. Make sure one of the sentences uses a linking verb that is not a form of "to be." Don't forget to circle the linking verbs!

1. _____

2. _____

3. _____

Action Verb or Linking Verb?

Linking Verb
Billy **sounded** strange last night.

Action Verb
I **sounded** the alarm in the middle of the night!

Pro Tip:
Some words can be action verbs or linking verbs depending on how they're used.

Let's practice!

Instructions:
Circle the verb in each of the following sentences and indicate whether it is an action verb or a linking verb.

EXAMPLE:
Unfortunately, that milk (tastes) rotten to me.   linking verb

1.   The beanstalk grew higher than the clouds!   _____

2.   At the end of a long night, the waiter looked exhausted.   _____

3.   Evelyn felt incredibly satisfied at the end of her presentation.   _____

4.   For quality assurance, I always taste my cookies.   _____

5.   I felt between the couch cushions for my lost wallet.   _____

Your turn!

Instructions:
Write sentences using the verbs below as action verbs or linking verbs as indicated. Don't forget to circle the verb in the sentence!

1.   smell (action) _____

2.   smell (linking) _____

3.   grow (linking) _____

Irregular Past Tense Verbs

That boy **sold** his grandfather's old hat!

Fran repeatedly **rang** my doorbell.

I **shot** hundreds of pictures with my new camera.

sell ➔ sold

ring ➔ rang

shoot ➔ shot

Pro Tip:
An irregular past tense verb is a past tense verb that is not formed by putting -d or -ed after the present tense verb.

Let's practice!

Instructions:
Circle the correct form of the past tense verb in parentheses.

EXAMPLE:

I was upset when I discovered that my sister (spent, spended) all my money on gum.

1. The sailor (standed, stood) resolutely on the bow of his ship.

2. Our wedding photographer (took, taked) thousands of pictures of our wedding.

3. We all (thinked, thought) that the movie was amazing.

4. Quinton never (meaned, meant) to hurt my feelings.

5. After receiving a parking ticket, Peter (writed, wrote) a check to pay the fine.

Your turn!

Instructions:
Write down the correct past tense verb form for each of the present tense verbs below.

stick	_____	ride	_____	see	_____
lose	_____	steal	_____	sing	_____
think	_____	teach	_____	make	_____

Writing with Verbs

INSTRUCTIONS (PART ONE):

Brainstorm some of your favorite action verbs and linking verbs. Make different lists for action verbs that express physical action and action verbs that express mental action.

PHYSICAL ACTION VERB	MENTAL ACTION VERB	LINKING VERB
------------------------------	------------------------------	------------------------------
------------------------------	------------------------------	------------------------------
------------------------------	------------------------------	------------------------------
------------------------------	------------------------------	------------------------------

INSTRUCTIONS (PART TWO):

Now choose TWO verbs from each of your categories and use them to write a short story. Don't forget to circle the verbs!

_____

_____

_____

_____

_____

_____

_____

The Big Verb Quiz!

INSTRUCTIONS: Indicate whether the <u>underlined verb</u> below is an action verb or a linking verb.

1. My manager <u>seemed</u> very happy when I told him what I had done.
   - ○ action verb   ○ linking verb

2. The magician suddenly <u>appeared</u> in the middle of the room.
   - ○ action verb   ○ linking verb

3. The magician <u>appeared</u> annoyed when kids in the audience started talking.
   - ○ action verb   ○ linking verb

4. The children all <u>looked</u> both ways before crossing the street.
   - ○ action verb   ○ linking verb

5. "<u>Stay</u> calm!" the firefighter yelled to the kitten stuck in the tree. "I'm coming!"
   - ○ action verb   ○ linking verb

INSTRUCTIONS: Indicate whether the <u>underlined action verb</u> below is transitive or intransitive.

6. The little bird <u>called</u> to her friends with a very specific song.
   - ○ transitive   ○ intransitive

7. The bully <u>called</u> me a name, but I ignored the insult.
   - ○ transitive   ○ intransitive

8. Students at my school <u>exit</u> through the iron gates at the end of the day.
   - ○ transitive   ○ intransitive

9. I <u>studied</u> my notes carefully all night before the big test.
   - ○ transitive   ○ intransitive

10. Garvey and her mother <u>played</u> video games together until bedtime.
    - ○ transitive   ○ intransitive

Meet the Adjectives!

I am an adjective!

I can modify a noun or a pronoun.

I tell what kind, which one, how many, or how much.

EXAMPLES

WHAT KIND: Henri painted an **_enormous_** landscape.

WHICH ONE: This is the **_first_** time I have ever sneezed.

HOW MANY: We invited about **_fifty_** people to the party.

HOW MUCH: Izzy likes her coffee with **_extra_** sugar.

Identifying Adjectives

My **new** apartment is just a **short** walk from the **nearest** subway.

That cat eats **less** kibble than the **other** one does.

Pro Tip:
An adjective modifies one or more nouns or pronouns. It can tell **what kind, which one, how many** (a number or quantity) or **how much** (an amount).

Let's Practice!

Instructions:
Circle all the adjectives in the following sentences.

EXAMPLE:
The art (historians) determined that the (expensive) painting wasn't (authentic).

1. The old port in the eastern part of town is lined with enormous factories.

2. Computer games can be surprisingly useful for teaching important skills.

3. Basketball is a fun sport that many people love to watch and play.

4. The powerful tornado resulted in much destruction and the loss of ten tons of corn.

5. The old carpet in the back bedroom smells like sautéed onions and rotten eggs.

Your turn!

Instructions:
Write sentences using more than one adjective in each sentence.
Don't forget to circle the adjectives!

1. _____

2. _____

3. _____

Words Adjectives Modify

Adjectives Before

Our new puppy ate a whole box of cookies.

Adjectives After

The puppy felt remorseful after eating all the cookies.

Pro Tip:
An adjective can come **before** or **after** the word or words it modifies.

Let's Practice!

Instructions:
Circle all of the adjectives in each of the following sentences.
Then draw an arrow from each adjective to the word it modifies.

EXAMPLE:
Dayton was excited when his sister gave him the latest game.

1. The old house smelled dank and musty.

2. If you order a large milkshake, be sure to get some extra spoons.

3. A flat surface is essential if you want to play marbles.

4. Many children enjoy the taste of banana pudding.

5. Will you be visiting your childhood home next week?

Your turn!

Instructions:
Write sentences using the adjectives below to describe a noun or pronoun. Circle each adjective and draw an arrow to the word it modifies.

1. purple _____

2. favorite _____

3. stinky _____

Demonstrative, Possessive, and Interrogative Adjectives

Demonstrative
This house belongs to my sister.

Possessive
_My_ sister asked me to invite you over to _her_ house.

Interrogative
On _which_ street is your sister's house?

Pro Tip:
A **demonstrative** adjective shows whether the noun it modifies is singular or plural and whether it is near or far.

A **possessive** adjective modifies a noun, showing possession or ownership.

An **interrogative** adjective is used to ask a question about a noun.

Let's Practice!

Instructions:
In each of the following sentences, draw an arrow from <u>underlined</u> adjective to the word it modifies. Then indicate whether the adjective is demonstrative, possessive, or interrogative.

EXAMPLE:
Please pay special attention to <u>these</u> important instructions.   demonstrative

1. <u>What</u> is your favorite breed of dog?   _____

2. I'm pretty sure <u>those</u> shoes are too expensive.   _____

3. Sasha and <u>her</u> little brother always drink milk in the morning.   _____

4. Those kids thought that <u>their</u> other school was better.   _____

5. <u>That</u> answer, I'm afraid, is unacceptable.   _____

Your turn!

Instructions:
Write a sentence using the adjectives below as demonstrative (D), possessive (P), or interrogative (I). Circle the adjectives and draw arrows to the words they modify.

1. his (P) _____

2. whose (I) _____

3. that (D) _____

Comparative and Superlative Adjectives

Comparative
Of these two cats, the golden one is <u>friendlier</u> and <u>**more cuddly**</u>.

Superlative
Of all the kittens in the entire shelter, I chose the <u>**friendliest**</u> and <u>**most cuddly**</u>.

Pro Tip:
A *comparative adjective* is used to make a comparison between two nouns or pronouns and is made by adding *-er* or by using the word **more**.

Pro Tip:
A *superlative adjective* is used to describe an extreme quality among three or more nouns or pronouns and is made by adding *-est* or by using the word **most**.

Let's Practice!

Instructions:
In the sentences below, draw an arrow from the <u>underlined adjective</u> to the word it modifies. Then indicate whether the adjective is comparative or superlative.

EXAMPLE:

Your room is <u>noisier</u> than it was yesterday.   <u>comparative</u>

1.   We happened to stop at the <u>**busiest**</u> intersection in the city.   _____

2.   I think that ferrets are the <u>**most interesting**</u> animals in the world.   _____

3.   My watch is <u>**more accurate**</u> than yours.   _____

4.   That is the <u>loudest</u> bear I have ever heard!   _____

5.   Your teacher is much <u>nicer</u> than I thought she'd be.   _____

Your turn!

Instructions:
Write sentences turning the adjectives below into comparative (C) or superlative (S) adjectives as indicated. Don't forget to circle the adjectives!

1.   funny (S) _____

2.   tasty (C) _____

3.   happy (S) _____

4.   blue (C) _____

Writing with Adjectives

INSTRUCTIONS (PART ONE):

Brainstorm a list of adjectives you might use to describe each of the nouns below.

1. puppy	2. view	3. store	4. plan
-------------------------	-------------------------	-------------------------	-------------------------
-------------------------	-------------------------	-------------------------	-------------------------
-------------------------	-------------------------	-------------------------	-------------------------
-------------------------	-------------------------	-------------------------	-------------------------

INSTRUCTIONS (PART TWO):

Write a story that incorporates the nouns and adjectives above. Circle the adjectives when you use them!

_____

_____

_____

_____

_____

_____

The Big Adjective Quiz!

INSTRUCTIONS: Indicate whether the underlined adjective tells what kind, which one, how many, or how much.

1. Everyone knows that I am a <u>happier</u> person now that I can play the piano.
   - ○ what kind
   - ○ which one
   - ○ how many
   - ○ how much

2. Whenever Susan orders tacos, she always says, "<u>No</u> cilantro, please."
   - ○ what kind
   - ○ which one
   - ○ how many
   - ○ how much

3. Roblox and Minecraft are my <u>two</u> favorite video games.
   - ○ what kind
   - ○ which one
   - ○ how many
   - ○ how much

4. <u>That</u> person doesn't really know what he's talking about.
   - ○ what kind
   - ○ which one
   - ○ how many
   - ○ how much

5. The whole class complained when we heard the <u>piercing</u> sound.
   - ○ what kind
   - ○ which one
   - ○ how many
   - ○ how much

INSTRUCTIONS: Identify the word the <u>underlined adjective</u> modifies from among the available options.

6. We all yelped when we hit the <u>long</u>, steep drop on the park's new rollercoaster.
   - ○ rollercoaster
   - ○ drop
   - ○ steep
   - ○ new

7. The little puppy seemed so sad and <u>helpless</u> when he walked into the room.
   - ○ puppy
   - ○ sad
   - ○ room
   - ○ little

8. My dad works for the school, but he does <u>occasional</u> baking jobs on the side.
   - ○ dad
   - ○ school
   - ○ jobs
   - ○ baking

9. The Broncos are my absolute <u>favorite</u> football team in the whole league.
   - ○ Broncos
   - ○ team
   - ○ football
   - ○ league

10. Our office is hot and <u>smelly</u>, but it's right across the street from a great restaurant.
    - ○ street
    - ○ restaurant
    - ○ hot
    - ○ office

Grammaropolis

Meet the Adverbs!

EXAMPLES

MODIFYING A VERB: Come <u>here</u>, and do it <u>quickly</u>!

MODIFYING AN ADJECTIVE: I feel <u>very</u> happy right now.

MODIFYING ANOTHER ADVERB: Your sister looked at me <u>somewhat</u> angrily.

Identifying Adverbs

Modifying Verbs
We studied <u>intensely</u>.

"intensely" modifies the verb "studied" and tells how.

Modifying Adjectives
Susan was <u>not</u> pleased with me.

"not" modifies the adjective "pleased" and tells to what extent (how much).

Pro Tip:
*An **adverb** modifies a verb, adjective, or other adverb. It can tell more nouns or pronouns. It can tell how, when, where or to what extent (how much).*

Modifying Other Adverbs
She raised her hand <u>very</u> high.

"very" modifies the adverb "high" and tells to what extent (how much).

Let's Practice!

Instructions:
Circle all of the adverbs in the following sentences.

EXAMPLE:
You should (never) eat (completely) dry crackers.

1. Please read your book carefully before you take the test tomorrow.

2. I will always love really cold ice cream.

3. We kept the windows open even though the angry dog barked constantly.

4. Your desk too cluttered to be very useful as a study environment.

5. My youngest daughter always smiles wide whenever she sees me.

Your turn!

Instructions:
Write sentences of your own using adverbs to modify verbs, adjectives, or other adverbs. Don't forget to circle the adverbs you use!

1. _____

2. _____

3. _____

Where
Come **home** by midnight.

When
I have **never** understood why some people hate checkers.

How
My dog panted **heavily** after retrieving the ball.

Pro Tip:
An adverb can tell **where, when, or how** an action happens.

Let's practice!

Instructions:
Circle the adverb in each of the following sentences and indicate whether it is telling "where," "when," or "how" an action happens.

EXAMPLE:

(Sometimes) I wonder if you're going to be nice to me.   <u>when</u>

1. I would like to see your new essay tomorrow.   _____

2. That cricket chirped loudly throughout the entire movie.   _____

3. Do you always brush your teeth in the dark?   _____

4. I slept unevenly last night, so my neck hurts.   _____

5. Sally will meet you there before the end of school.   _____

Your turn!

Instructions:
Write sentences below using adverbs to tell where, when, or how an action happens. Don't forget to circle the adverbs when you use them.

1. where   _____

2. when   _____

3. how   _____

Words Adverbs Modify

Adverb Before

Alvin <u>expertly</u> hopped down the stairs two at a time.

Adverb After

Alvin hopped <u>expertly</u> down the stairs two at a time.

Pro Tip:
An adverb can come **before** *or* **after** *the word it modifies.*

Let's practice!

Instructions:
Circle all of the adverbs in each of the following sentences. Then draw an arrow from each adverb to the word it modifies.

EXAMPLE:
Fernando (definitely) feels (strongly) that you and I deserve a bowl of pudding.

1. "I am extremely satisfied," said the customer pleasantly to the clerk.

2. If you work hard, you might go far in life.

3. We must leave soon, so I need you to look carefully for any missing items.

4. "Is it possible to whisper loudly?" I whispered loudly to my friend in the movie theater.

5. My car is really fast, so we can go home quickly.

Your turn!

Instructions:
Write sentences using the adverbs below. Circle each adverb and draw an arrow to the word it modifies.

1. angrily _____

2. always _____

3. totally _____

Comparative and Superlative Adverbs

Comparative
The ball landed <u>nearer</u> to me than to you. That's why I acted **more quickly** than you did.

Superlative
The ball landed <u>nearest</u> to me than to anyone else. That's why I acted the **most quickly** of all.

Pro Tip:
A **comparative adverb** is used to compare two things and is made by adding -er or by using the word **more**.

Pro Tip:
A **superlative adverb** indicates an extreme quality in a comparison and is made by adding -est or by using the word **most**.

Let's Practice!

Instructions:
In each of the following sentences, draw an arrow from <u>underlined adverb</u> to the word it modifies. Then indicate whether the adverb is comparative or superlative.

EXAMPLE:

I promise you that nobody works <u>harder</u> than I do.   _____comparative_____

1. Gerald knocked **more loudly** the second time he knocked.   _____

2. The baseball player hit the ball the **farthest** of anyone.   _____

3. I tiptoed **more quietly** than Billy, which is why he got caught.   _____

4. That drummer plays the **loudest** of anyone I have ever heard.   _____

5. My friend entered the room **more confidently** than I did.   _____

Your turn!

Instructions:
Write sentences turning the adverbs below into comparative (C) or superlative (S) adverbs as indicated. Don't forget to circle the adverb!

1. carefully (S) _____

2. lightly (C) _____

3. brightly (C) _____

4. early (S) _____

Writing with Adverbs

INSTRUCTIONS (PART ONE):
Create adverbs that tell "how" by incorporating -ly to the end of the adjectives below.

ADJECTIVE	ADVERB
1. busy	1.
2. quick	2.
3. sly	3.
4. sad	4.
5. bright	5.

INSTRUCTIONS (PART TWO):
Fill in the blanks with your favorite adverbs that tell "where" and "when."

WHERE

1.

2.

WHEN

1.

2.

INSTRUCTIONS (PART THREE):
Write a story that incorporates all of the adverbs above. Circle the adverbs when you use them!

_____

_____

_____

_____

_____

_____

The Big Adverb Quiz!

INSTRUCTIONS: Identify the adverb in each of the sentences below from the available options.

1. My good friend briefly introduced me before I gave my acceptance speech.
   - ○ acceptance
   - ○ introduced
   - ○ me
   - ○ briefly

2. The actor paced nervously before his entrance onto the stage.
   - ○ before
   - ○ onto
   - ○ nervously
   - ○ paced

3. The kids who live across from me never eat chocolate cake.
   - ○ live
   - ○ never
   - ○ across
   - ○ eat

4. This class is the absolute best class you can take at this school.
   - ○ This
   - ○ best
   - ○ absolute
   - ○ is

5. Lyndon usually bikes to work, but today he decided to walk.
   - ○ bikes
   - ○ decided
   - ○ walk
   - ○ today

INSTRUCTIONS: Indicate whether the <u>underlined adverbs</u> below tell where, when, or how.

6. The teacher <u>stubbornly</u> refused to change my grade from a B to an A.
   - ○ where
   - ○ when
   - ○ how

7. The funny thing about chocolate is that I <u>always</u> find myself wanting more of it.
   - ○ where
   - ○ when
   - ○ how

8. If you ever feel like running <u>home</u> after school, I think you should walk instead.
   - ○ where
   - ○ when
   - ○ how

9. I raised my hand as high as I could, and I volunteered <u>whole-heartedly</u> for the job.
   - ○ where
   - ○ when
   - ○ how

10. "Johnny," said Felix, "<u>sometimes</u> I have absolutely no idea what you're thinking.
    - ○ where
    - ○ when
    - ○ how

Grammaropolis

EXAMPLES

WITHOUT PRONOUNS: <u>Dayton</u> read <u>a book</u> to <u>Julie, Peter, Albert, LaTasha, Gerald, Bob, and me.</u>

WITH PRONOUNS: <u>He</u> read <u>it</u> to <u>us</u>.

Why We Use Pronouns

Without Pronouns
Julia's brother gave Julia a toy roadrunner, but Julia's brother still wanted Julia to share the toy roadrunner with Julia's brother.

With Pronouns
Julia's brother gave _her_ a toy roadrunner, but _he_ still wanted _her_ to share _it_ with _him_.

Pro Tip:
We use pronouns so that nouns or other pronouns in the sentence don't have to be repeated.

Let's practice!

Instructions:
Fill in the blanks in the sentences below using the pronouns that make sense.

EXAMPLE:
Jason and Franklin wanted their teacher to give __them__ really good grades.

1. Dogs are fun to play with. _____ always seem to be in a good mood.

2. Bernie gave me a dollar, but then _____ asked _____ to give it back to _____.

3. My mother and I went to the store, where _____ bought vanilla cake mix.

4. I know that Zeke doesn't like that song because _____ can't stop talking about _____.

5. There are instructions on the side of this box. Please follow _____ very carefully.

Your turn!

Instructions:
Write a short sentence using no pronouns. Then write the same sentence replacing the nouns with pronouns. Don't forget to circle the pronouns!

_____

_____

Pronouns and Antecedents

Pro Tip:
The word (or words) that the pronoun replaces is called the antecedent.

Let's practice!

Instructions:
Circle the pronoun in each of the following sentences and draw an arrow to the word it replaces.

EXAMPLE:

My father-in-law loves salty foods. He puts extra salt on everything.

1. The boy down the street loves skateboarding. He practices every afternoon.

2. Gavin and Constance went to a movie last night, and they enjoyed every minute.

3. "Susan," my mother said. "You need to wash the dishes before bedtime!"

4. This desk is not very comfortable because it is really wobbly.

5. Mrs. Johnson is my favorite teacher. She absolutely loves puppies.

Your turn!

Instructions:
Write sentences using the word pairs below as the pronoun and antecedent. Then circle the pronoun and draw an arrow to the antecedent.

1. girls/they _____

2. brother/he _____

3. Dalia/she _____

Subjective and Objective Pronouns

Subjective Pronouns
<u>She</u> enjoys sunsets.
<u>We</u> love to play checkers.
<u>They</u> never pay attention to Hank.

Objective Pronouns
Show <u>her</u> the sunset!
Play checkers with <u>us</u>.
Hank isn't paying attention to <u>them</u> either.

Pro Tip:
A subjective pronoun acts as the **subject** of the sentence.

Pro Tip:
An objective pronoun acts as the **object** of the sentence.

Let's Practice!

Instructions:
Circle the pronoun in each of the sentences below and indicate whether it is subjective or objective pronoun.

EXAMPLE:

(You) should make sure that the dog takes his medicine.   subjective

1. Chandler wants to sing you a song today.   _____

2. Last night, we took all of our friends to the race track.   _____

3. Janet called. Tell her that the move starts soon.   _____

4. No matter what they say, this book is fantastic.   _____

5. Please hand this to your little brother's best friend.   _____

Your turn!

Instructions:
Write sentences using the pronouns below. Circle the pronouns when you use them and write S for subjective and O for objective above the circles.

1. him _____

2. them _____

3. I _____

4. we _____

Name: _____

Intensive and Reflexive Pronouns

Intensive Pronouns
I **myself** ate those cookies.
Henry did the homework **himself**.

Reflexive Pronouns
I baked **myself** those cookies.
Henry made **himself** do his homework.

Pro Tip:
An **intensive** pronoun emphasizes, or intensifies, a noun or another pronoun.

Pro Tip:
A **reflexive** pronoun directs the action of the verb back to the subject of the sentence.

Let's Practice!

Instructions:
In each of the following sentences, indicate whether <u>underlined pronoun</u> is intensive or reflexive and draw an arrow to its antecedent.

EXAMPLE:
You should definitely make **yourself** go to bed earlier.   _reflexive_

1. You **yourself** are the only person that matters to me.   _____

2. Fiona decorated this entire room **herself**.   _____

3. We bought **ourselves** an expensive cookie to share.   _____

4. I watched as my teammates prepared **themselves** for the big game.   _____

5. Devon calmed **himself** down by taking some deep breaths.   _____

Your turn!

Instructions:
Write sentences using the pronouns below as indicated: (R) for reflexive and (I) for intensive. Circle each pronoun and draw an arrow to its antecedent.

1. yourself (R) _____

2. ourselves (I) _____

3. myself (R) _____

Grammaropolis

Pronoun or Adjective?

Adjective
I would love to bake **some** cookies when we get home tonight.

Pronoun
I love cookies! Please may I have **some**?

Pro Tip:
Some words can be either pronouns or adjectives, depending on how they're used in the sentence.

Let's Practice!

Instructions:
Indicate whether the <u>underlined word</u> is an adjective or a pronoun. If it is an adjective, draw an arrow to the word it modifies. If it is a pronoun, draw an arrow to the word it replaces.

EXAMPLE:

<u>**Those**</u> people are the nicest people I have ever met.   _____adjective_____

1. Somebody needs to remind <u>**her**</u> that this is not a roller rink.   _____

2. Did you know that <u>**these**</u> are my favorite shoes in the world?   _____

3. There is some chocolate in the cupboard. Do you want <u>**any**</u>?   _____

4. Give me <u>**that**</u> pencil back right now!   _____

5. Listen to this: pulling hair is not allowed in <u>**this**</u> classroom.   _____

Your turn!

Instructions:
Write sentences using the words below as indicated: (A) for adjective and (P) for pronoun. Don't forget to circle the word in each sentence.

1. this (P) _____

2. that (P) _____

3. her (A) _____

4. any (A) _____

Writing with Pronouns

Name:

INSTRUCTIONS (PART ONE):
Brainstorm four people and list their corresponding pronouns, and then brainstorm four things and list their corresponding pronouns. Remember that your pronouns can be subjective or objective!

	PERSON	PRONOUN		THING	PRONOUN
1.	doctor	/ she	1.	broccoli	/ it
2.		/	2.		/
3.		/	3.		/
4.		/	4.		/
5.		/	5.		/

INSTRUCTIONS (PART TWO):
Now write a story that incorporates at least two of the people and at least two of the things from your lists above. Remember to use both the pronouns *and* the antecedents! Circle the pronouns when you use them.

_____

_____

_____

_____

_____

_____

The Big Pronoun Quiz!

INSTRUCTIONS: Identify the antecedent (the word the <u>underlined pronoun</u> replaces) from the options below.

1. The insect hides <u>itself</u> by turning the same color as the leaf.
   ○ color   ○ leaf   ○ insect   ○ hides

2. Those shoes are <u>mine</u>, but I am sure that if you ask Billy, he will let you borrow his.
   ○ Billy   ○ his   ○ I   ○ shoes

3. Charles took a nap in the woods, and when <u>he</u> woke up, he'd forgotten where he was.
   ○ Charles   ○ woods   ○ nap   ○ he

4. The teacher loves her students so much that she would do anything to help <u>them</u>.
   ○ teacher   ○ anything   ○ so   ○ students

5. The thunderstorm ended just as suddenly as <u>it</u> had begun.
   ○ thunderstorm   ○ begun   ○ it   ○ ended

INSTRUCTIONS: Indicate whether the <u>underlined pronouns</u> below are reflexive or intensive.

6. Janelle is a carpenter, and she built all of the cabinets in here <u>herself</u>.
   ○ reflexive   ○ intensive

7. Being a person who is nice to other people is how Jamie defines <u>himself</u>.
   ○ reflexive   ○ intensive

8. I inspired <u>myself</u> to write a poem every day.
   ○ reflexive   ○ intensive

9. You <u>yourself</u> are the best friend a guy could ever hope for.
   ○ reflexive   ○ intensive

10. Sometimes I like to watch the lizards sun <u>themselves</u> on the big rock out back.
    ○ reflexive   ○ intensive

Grammaropolis

EXAMPLES

JOINING WORDS: I ate so many cookies **_and_** brownies at your birthday party.

JOINING PHRASES: I usually only eat cookies in the school lunchroom **_or_** at my father's house.

JOINING CLAUSES: Your cookies looked spectacular, **_so_** I decided to give them a try!

Coordinating Conjunctions

Words
Do you prefer blue <u>or</u> green?

Phrases
I piled my plate high with fresh strawberries <u>and</u> ripe bananas.

Complete Thoughts
The sun is shining, <u>yet</u> it's still very cold outside.

Pro Tip:
The FANBOYS (also known as coordinating conjunctions) are used to join words, phrases, or complete thoughts (independent clauses).

Let's practice!

Instructions:
Circle all of the coordinating conjunctions in the sentences below.

EXAMPLE:

Phones (and) computers are recent inventions, (yet) I can't imagine life without them.

1. I am sad, for I can't find my new dog.

2. The building is old and rundown, so I'm afraid to step inside.

3. Fernando doesn't enjoy hamburgers, nor does he enjoy cheeseburgers.

4. You can run to the store, or I can drive you there.

5. Salt and pepper can be overused, but this dish is perfect!

Your turn!

Instructions:
Write sentences using the following conjunctions to join words or word groups. Don't forget to circle the conjunction in the sentence!

1. but _____

2. and _____

3. for _____

Correlative Conjunctions

Pro Tip:
A *correlative* conjunction is a two-part conjunction used to join words or phrases used in the same way.

Pro Tip:
Common correlative conjunctions are *either/or, neither/nor, whether/or,* and *not only/but also.*

Let's Practice!

Instructions:
Circle both parts of the correlative conjunction in each of the following sentences and draw a line linking the two parts.

EXAMPLE:

I didn't know (whether) to smile (or) to frown for the picture.

1. Jayden wants to play either basketball or badminton this year.

2. Both the dog and the cat are afraid of the gusty weather outside.

3. My mother is not only a family doctor but also a race car driver.

4. You should feel free to order either pancakes or waffles this morning.

5. My guess is that school is going to happen whether we want it to or not.

Your turn!

Instructions:
Write complete sentences using the correlative conjunctions below. Don't forget to circle and link both parts!

1. either/or _____

2. both/and _____

3. neither/nor _____

Subordinating Conjunctions

Subordinate Clause First

Because it stopped raining, we can go out to play!

Whenever I see someone in pain, my heart hurts.

Subordinate Clause Second

We can go out to play **because** it stopped raining!

My heart hurts **whenever** I see someone in pain.

Pro Tip:
A *subordinating conjunction* introduces a subordinate, or dependent, clause.

Pro Tip:
The subordinate clause can come before or after the independent clause.

Let's Practice!

Instructions:
Circle the subordinating conjunction in each of the following sentences and then underline the entire subordinate clause.

EXAMPLE:
<u>(Once) the play starts</u>, everyone will have to be very quiet.

1. My dentist said I don't need braces anymore now that my teeth are straight.

2. After the movie ended, we all sat in our seats unable to move.

3. Omar hasn't eaten salad since he broke his tooth on an olive pit.

4. Although it doesn't seem like it, that ferret is the friendliest animal in town.

5. Wherever you see smoke, there's bound to be fire.

Your turn!

Instructions:
Write complete sentences using each of the subordinating conjunctions below to introduce a subordinate clause. Don't forget to circle the conjunction and underline the entire subordinate clause!

1. if _____

2. before _____

3. unless _____

Identifying Conjunctions

> **Without Conjunctions**
> Annie likes cats. She likes dogs. Anne found her favorite cat at a shelter. Annie likes to rescue animals.

> **With Conjunctions**
> Annie likes cats **and** dogs, **and** she found her favorite cat at a shelter **because** she likes to rescue animals.

Pro Tip:
Conjunctions make it possible to link words and ideas together in many different ways.

Let's Practice!

Instructions:
Circle all of the conjunctions in each of the following sentences.

EXAMPLE:

Whenever I see a scary movie, I always cover my ears and close my eyes.

1. I not only laughed but cried when my sausage fell on the floor.

2. Before you make your decision, I want you to think long and hard.

3. Enrique is not only my best friend but also a world champion in hacky sack.

4. Sandra is anxious, for her team is playing in the championship game today.

5. Neither Dawn nor David has any idea that I can sing and dance.

Your turn!

Instructions:
Write sentences that incorporate each of the words below as conjunctions.
Don't forget to circle the conjunctions!

1. after _____

2. yet _____

3. either/or _____

Writing with Conjunctions

INSTRUCTIONS (PART ONE):
Circle THREE coordinating conjunctions, TWO correlative conjunctions, and TWO subordinating conjunctions from among the choices below.

COORDINATING

for
and
nor
but
or
yet
so

CORRELATIVE

either/or
neither/nor
not only/but also
both/and
whether/or

SUBORDINATING

after	even if	though
although	even though	unless
as	if	until
because	now that	whenever
before	once	wherever
by the time	since	while
	so	

INSTRUCTIONS (PART TWO):
Now write a story that incorporates the conjunctions you have circled. Remember to circle the conjunctions once you use them in the story as well!

_____

_____

_____

_____

_____

_____

_____

The Big Conjunction Quiz!

INSTRUCTIONS: Indicate the correct type of conjunction for each of the <u>underlined conjunctions</u> below.

1. Everyone I know wants to be a movie star, <u>yet</u> nobody wants to put in the work.
   O coordinating   O correlative   O subordinating

2. Watson found that <u>neither</u> spinach <u>nor</u> asparagus made his tummy upset.
   O coordinating   O correlative   O subordinating

3. <u>After</u> you brush your teeth, you can turn out the light and go to bed.
   O coordinating   O correlative   O subordinating

4. You have to start doing your homework, <u>or</u> you will lose your allowance.
   O coordinating   O correlative   O subordinating

5. The moon is out, <u>so</u> I can't see the stars very well.
   O coordinating   O correlative   O subordinating

6. Jacques likes his ice cream with <u>both</u> chocolate sauce <u>and</u> whipped cream.
   O coordinating   O correlative   O subordinating

7. The lights went out all over town, <u>for</u> there was a malfunction at the power plant.
   O coordinating   O correlative   O subordinating

8. Kevin smiles <u>whenever</u> he sees his friend walking down the street.
   O coordinating   O correlative   O subordinating

9. <u>As soon as</u> I finish this lesson, I will run into the yard screaming happily.
   O coordinating   O correlative   O subordinating

10. This may be hard for you to hear, <u>but</u> your brother is from outer space.
    O coordinating   O correlative   O subordinating

Grammaropolis

Meet the Prepositions!

I am a preposition!

I show the relationship between the object (a noun or pronoun) and other words in the sentence.

EXAMPLES

WHERE: I hung the painting <u>**on**</u> the wall <u>**behind**</u> the door.

WHEN: Grover will draw you a painting <u>**after**</u> supper.

LOGICAL: I only play card games <u>**according to**</u> the rules.

Identifying Prepositions

Space (where)
I stepped **inside** the room.

Time (when)
Navid will be here **until** nightfall.

Logical Relationship
I prefer my ice cream **with** sprinkles.

Pro Tip:
A preposition locates an object in **time** or **space** or shows a **logical relationship** between the object and the rest of the sentence.

Pro Tip:
A preposition that is more than one word but acts as a single preposition is called a **compound preposition.** Examples include: **next to, instead of, because of,** and **due to.**

Let's practice!

Instructions:
Circle the prepositions in the following sentences and then indicate whether they help tell when or where the action of the verb happens or if they show a logical relationship. Don't forget to look for compound prepositions!

EXAMPLE:

I am doing this all (for) your benefit.   ___logical___

1.   The plane was undetectable as it flew below radar.   _____

2.   This is the best day of my life.   _____

3.   I was so happy that I easily jumped over the fence.   _____

4.   Yolanda set her guitar down, leaning it gently against the wall. _____

5.   Do you want to eat before the show?   _____

Your turn!

Instructions:
Finish the sentences below by incorporating your own prepositions. Don't forget to circle the prepositions!

1.   <u>Someone shouted</u> _____

2.   <u>Veronica and Daniela looked</u> _____

3.   <u>Baxter's dog ran</u> _____

Prepositional Phrases

A preposition is placed at the beginning of a prepositional phrase.

near the school

during class

Pro Tip:
A prepositional phrase starts with a preposition and ends with the object of the preposition.

Let's practice!

Instructions:
In each of the following sentences, underline the entire prepositional phrase and circle the preposition. There may be more than one!

EXAMPLE:
I learned all (of) the rules (in) the book (apart from) rule number seven.

1. I peeked inside the window of the house across the street.

2. Someone hit the ball over the fence and right into Mrs. Welton's yard.

3. According to Bobby, that's the whole point of the game.

4. I haven't seen him since last Tuesday at noon.

5. Lexi wrote a note with disappearing ink and gave it to her friend.

Your turn!

Instructions:
Write sentences that incorporate the prepositional phrases below. Remember to underline the prepositional phrases and circle the prepositions.

1. before sunset _____

2. with a sponge _____

3. down the street _____

Preposition or Adverb?

Adverb
We tossed the dirty sock <u>out</u>.
"out" is by itself, without the rest of a phrase. That means it's an adverb.

Preposition
We tossed the dirty sock <u>out the window</u>.
"out the window" is a prepositional phrase, so out is a preposition.

Pro Tip:
Some words can be used as either prepositions or adverbs. Remember that a preposition always has to be at the front of the phrase. If there's no phrase, it's not a preposition!

Let's Practice!

Instructions:
Indicate whether the <u>underlined word</u> is a preposition or an adverb. If it is a preposition, draw an arrow to the object of the phrase. If it is an adverb, draw an arrow to the word it modifies.

EXAMPLE:
My mom kissed me on the forehead after she tucked me <u>in</u>.   _____adverb_____

1. I clutched my favorite necklace tightly <u>in</u> my hand.   _____

2. As soon as the lights went <u>down</u>, the audience clapped.   _____

3. Harlan wandered <u>down</u> the street with nowhere to go.   _____

4. We did everything we could to get <u>up</u> the mountain first.   _____

5. If you don't look <u>up</u> occasionally, you're bound to trip.   _____

Your turn!

Instructions:
Write sentences using the words below as adverbs (A) or prepositions (P) as indicated. If it is a preposition, draw an arrow to the object of the phrase. If it is an adverb, draw an arrow to the word it modifies.

1. by (A) _____

2. by (P) _____

3. around (P) _____

4. around (A) _____

Writing with Prepositions

Name:

INSTRUCTIONS (PART ONE):
Create six prepositional phrases with the prepositions below. Be sure to use at least one compound preposition.

SINGLE WORD PREPOSITIONS   COMPOUND PREPOSITIONS

above	behind	down	near	through		according to
across	below	during	off	throughout		ahead of
after	beneath	from	on	to		apart from
against	beside	in	out	toward		due to
around	between	inside	outside	under		because of
at	beyond	into	over	until		next to
before	by		since	upon		resulting in

1._____   4._____

2._____   5._____

3._____   6._____

INSTRUCTIONS (PART TWO):
Now write a story that incorporates the prepositions you have circled. Remember to circle the prepositions once you use them in the story as well!

_____

_____

_____

_____

_____

_____

The Big Preposition Quiz!

INSTRUCTIONS: Indicate whether the <u>underlined prepositions</u> below help tell where, when, or show a logical relationship.

1. I do my best to live <u>with</u> an optimistic attitude.
   ○ where ○ when ○ logical relationship

2. There's nothing I want more than for you to spend the night <u>at</u> my house.
   ○ where ○ when ○ logical relationship

3. I carefully laid the wreath <u>upon</u> my grandfather's doorstep.
   ○ where ○ when ○ logical relationship

4. So many classes were canceled this year <u>due to</u> complications with the technology.
   ○ where ○ when ○ logical relationship

5. You're not supposed to finish your homework <u>during</u> class.
   ○ where ○ when ○ logical relationship

INSTRUCTIONS: Indicate whether the <u>underlined words</u> below are prepositions or an adverbs.

6. Someone fell <u>down</u> and made a loud noise, but it wasn't me.
   ○ preposition ○ adverb

7. I have never met that guy <u>before</u>.
   ○ preposition ○ adverb

8. Henry knew that he had to go to bed <u>before</u> midnight.
   ○ preposition ○ adverb

9. "I've never been here," said Delilah. "What's the harm in taking a peek <u>inside</u>?"
   ○ preposition ○ adverb

10. The funny thing is that I looked <u>around</u> the entire room before I saw you.
    ○ preposition ○ adverb

Grammaropolis

Meet the Interjections!

EXAMPLES

MILD EMOTION: <u>Nope</u>, I've never been there.

STRONG EMOTION: <u>No</u>! I don't want to go there!

Identifying Interjections

Mild Emotion
<u>Man</u>, I honestly don't know the answer to that question.

Strong Emotion
<u>Drat</u>! I just dropped hot sauce all over my toe.

Pro Tip:
Mild emotion is set apart with a **comma**.
Strong emotion is set apart with an **exclamation mark**.

Let's practice!

Instructions:
Circle the interjection in each of the following sentences and indicate whether it is expressing mild or strong emotion.

EXAMPLE:

Oooh, that's a scary ghost right there.   _____mild_____

1.   "Hmm," she said. "Now that you mention it, I do like fries."   _____

2.   Egads! That's quite the recipe you want me to make.   _____

3.   Nah, I don't think now is the time for handstands.   _____

4.   Yay! My favorite author just released a new book!   _____

5.   Boo! Did I scare you even just a little bit?   _____

Your turn!

Instructions:
Write sentences using the interjections below to express mild or strong emotion, as indicated.

1.   Oh (mild)   _____

2.   Oh (strong)   _____

3.   Yeah (strong)   _____

Writing with Interjections

INSTRUCTIONS (PART ONE):
Write down ten interjections you might use to express mild or strong emotion. Feel free to make up a few of them if you want! Circle your six favorite ones.

1._____   6._____

2._____   7._____

3._____   8._____

4._____   9._____

5._____   10._____

INSTRUCTIONS (PART TWO):
Now write sentences using your favorite interjections. Remember to use a comma when you express mild emotion and an exclamation mark with strong emotion!

MILD EMOTION

1. _____

2. _____

3. _____

STRONG EMOTION:

1. _____

2. _____

3. _____

Grammaropolis

The Big Interjection Quiz!

INSTRUCTIONS: Identify the interjection in each of the sentences below from among the available options.

1. Yes! I'm almost ready for the weekend to start!
   - ○ almost
   - ○ Yes
   - ○ start
   - ○ weekend

2. Oh, that sounds wonderful to me.
   - ○ wonderful
   - ○ me
   - ○ that
   - ○ Oh

3. Ah! I finally remembered why I should never pick up a hot plate without gloves.
   - ○ finally
   - ○ Ah
   - ○ never
   - ○ hot

4. "Hey!" said Mrs. Johnson. "You just threw your baseball into my yard."
   - ○ Hey
   - ○ You
   - ○ yard
   - ○ baseball

5. My appointment is on the third floor, and there's no elevator. Ugh.
   - ○ and
   - ○ no
   - ○ Ugh
   - ○ third

INSTRUCTIONS: Indicate whether the <u>underlined interjections</u> below express mild emotion or strong emotion.

6. <u>Yoo-hoo!</u> Dinner's ready!
   - ○ mild emotion
   - ○ strong emotion

7. <u>Mmm,</u> now that you mention it, I do think I'll need to wear a safety harness.
   - ○ mild emotion
   - ○ strong emotion

8. <u>Phew</u>! I didn't think we would ever get here.
   - ○ mild emotion
   - ○ strong emotion

9. <u>Ouch</u>! That box of rocks just fell on my foot!
   - ○ mild emotion
   - ○ strong emotion

10. <u>Well,</u> I'm not sure it's appropriate for clowns to do math like that.
    - ○ mild emotion
    - ○ strong emotion

Grammaropolis

The Big Quiz Answer Key!

NOUNS
1. compound
2. collective
3. proper
4. abstract
5. compound
6. plural
7. plural
8. singular
9. plural
10. plural

PRONOUNS
1. insect
2. shoes
3. Charles
4. students
5. thunderstorm
6. intensive
7. reflexive
8. reflexive
9. intensive
10. reflexive

VERBS
1. linking verb
2. action verb
3. linking verb
4. action verb
5. linking verb
6. intransitive
7. transitive
8. intransitive
9. transitive
10. transitive

CONJUNCTIONS
1. coordinating
2. correlative
3. subordinating
4. coordinating
5. coordinating
6. correlative
7. coordinating
8. subordinating
9. subordinating
10. coordinating

ADJECTIVES
1. what kind
2. how much
3. how many
4. which one
5. what kind
6. drop
7. puppy
8. jobs
9. team
10. office

PREPOSITIONS
1. logical
2. where
3. where
4. logical
5. when
6. adverb
7. adverb
8. preposition
9. adverb
10. preposition

ADVERBS
1. briefly
2. nervously
3. never
4. absolute
5. today
6. how
7. when
8. where
9. how
10. when

INTERJECTIONS
1. Yes
2. Oh
3. Ah
4. Hey
5. Ugh
6. strong
7. mild
8. strong
9. strong
10. mild

GRAMMAR CURRICULUM CHECKLIST

☑ Innovative and engaging

☑ Aligned to state standards

☑ Addresses various learning styles

☑ Created and refined in the ultimate proving grounds: the classroom

THE STORYBOOKS

4/24/2019 | $6.99
Paperback | 32 pages | 8" x 8"
Full-color illustrations throughout
Includes instructional back matter
Ages 7 to 11 | Grades 1 to 5
JUVENILE NONFICTION /
LANGUAGE ARTS / GRAMMAR

9781644420157 | Noun
9781644420171 | Verb
9781644420133 | Adjective
9781644420102 | Adverb
9781644420164 | Pronoun
9781644420119 | Conjunction
9781644420140 | Preposition
9781644420126 | Interjection

- An eight-book series starring the parts of speech, which are personified based on the roles they play in the sentence.

- Featuring a different character-based adventure for every part of speech.

- Each book includes standards–aligned definitions and examples, just like you'd find in a textbook (but way more fun).

THE WORKBOOKS

3/03/2020 | $12.99 | B&W
PB | 64 pages | 11"H x 8.5"W
Includes quizzes & instruction
Ages 7 to 11 | Grades 1 to 5
JUVENILE NONFICTION /
LANGUAGE ARTS / GRAMMAR

9781644420300 | Grade 1
9781644420317 | Grade 2
9781644420324 | Grade 3
9781644420331 | Grade 4
9781644420188 | Grade 5

- Skill-building workbooks featuring character-based instruction along with various comprehension checks and writing exercises.

- Aligned to Common Core and state standards for K–5.

Grammaropolis is available through Ingram Publisher Services.
Contact your IPS Sales Representative to order.
Call (866) 400-5351, Fax (800) 838-1149,
ips@ingramcontent.com, or visit ipage.

Printed in the USA
CPSIA information can be obtained
at www.ICGtesting.com
JSHW060239160824
68134JS00058BA/2678